MW00712500

# NO LONGER THE VICTIM

## Charles P. Roberson, Sr.

Christian Life Publishers
6007 Veterans Parkway
Columbus, GA 31909

Editor: Ca-Asia Shields
Graphic Design: Prof. H. Pernell
Johnson & Davonte James
Cover Design: Brittany Burns

ISBN: 978-0-9896554-4-6
For Worldwide Distribution
Printed in the U.S.A.

# TABLE OF CONTENTS

Chapter 1 Who Dropped You? .......... 11

Chapter 2 One-On-One with Grace ...... 23

Chapter 3 No Longer the Victim ........ 37

Chapter 4 Grace Looks Good on You .... 47

Chapter 5 Finally Confident! ........... 55

Chapter 6 Conclusion ................ 65

# DEDICATION

This book is dedicated to my dear father, Mr. Willie M. Roberson, Jr. Born in August, 1925, my father lived through some of the toughest times in American history. Even though times were tough and challenges were many, my father raised ten children and committed his life to improving his community. "Dad, I dedicate this book to you and your legacy; and I'm

"Putting My Best Foot Forward."

I must also give honor to my wife, my mother, my children, and the family at Kingdom Life Christian Fellowship in Savannah, GA. Over the past 24 years Yolanda and I have lived everyday together as best friends. We've walked through the pains and joys of life with an unfailing and unconditional love. She is my heartbeat. My mother, Mary, along with my father, taught me to serve God and always put Him first. Thank you, Mother, for always being my example of excellence. I am so blessed to have the greatest two children in the world, Charles Jr. and Channah. I am so proud of both of you, and I am who I am because of your love. Finally, I am extremely thankful for the love and support I receive from the members of Kingdom Life Christian Fellowship. Your love towards my family and me has been immeasurable.

# Special Acknowledgement

I must acknowledge some very special people who have been an invaluable, spiritual, and professional resource for me.

Bishop Vaughn McLaughlin of Potters House International Ministries, Jacksonville, FL, is my spiritual father.

Pastor Thomas E. Williams, Pastor of First African Baptist Church of East Savannah, GA, was my birthing Pastor; and he also led me to Christ.

Gwen David is my sister and writing inspiration.

# INTRODUCTION

This book is the result of much prayer and pain. I don't know if you know it or not, but prayer and pain are a winning mixture. Simply put, pain can be devastating, but prayer coupled with hope points us toward our future. My father is my hero and was the one person who inspired me to "put my best foot forward." On July 10, 2013, my father transitioned from time to eternity. A part of me left with him. In the days that followed, I asked every question in the book. "Why Lord?" "Why me Lord?" "Why us Lord?" "Why now Lord?" As I continued to ask questions, I started receiving answers. Before I reveal some of the answers I received, let me say that in life it's not just getting the right answers but asking the right questions. Some questions probe beneath the surface entering the deep core of what's really going on. I grew up thinking that we could not ask God questions. But one day I got the revelation that God is my Heavenly Father; and if I approach Him with reverence and respect, I could ask Him for anything I needed. So here I was after my natural father's death, asking my Heavenly Father questions that began with "Why." The first answer was, "My grace is sufficient for you."

*And he said unto me, my grace is sufficient for thee: for my strength is made perfect in weakness. Most gladly therefore will I rather glory in my infirmities, that the power of Christ may rest upon me (2 Cor. 12:9).*

Yes, I heard the answer, "Grace is Sufficient." I spent several days trying to put it all into proper context. After pondering on this I was able to understand that the answer included the secret of "perfect strength" that comes into our lives at a time of "overwhelming weakness." It is like the Lord reminded me that it's hard to ever be a VICTIM and be connected to Him. Even if something weakens you, His super-turbo burners of strength kick in.

As you are reading this book I am sure that you've been there before feeling like you were left alone, hurt, damaged, and victimized by something that happened in your life. The same answer that I received is available for you. Regardless of what you're facing, "His Grace is Sufficient for you."

This book represents a paradigm shift on how you view yourself. It is a reminder that in life you cannot always control what happens to you, but you play a major role in how you respond to it. It is my intention to call you into strength and bring you face to face with the Strength Giver. It is time to unfold your hands and take your life back. Massive damage requires massive repairs. Everything you need and every desire you have can be found in this season. Welcome to your post-victim life and to a time of discovery of new possibilities. God is able to make all grace abound toward you so much so that you will always have everything you need and plenty left over to share with others (2 Cor. 9:8).

I like to call it abounding grace, and what's amazing is that you get more than one serving.

This kind of grace grows and expands leaving you full of amazement. Hopefully, your palate is getting excited and you can smell the full course of freedom being prepared for you. Get ready to soar and get your vision back because this abounding grace is made for people like you and me who've been damaged by something.

The word abound means, "exist in large numbers or amounts." This book is directed right at the very thing that made you cry. It is my intention to say to any darkness that has held you that you are now abounding in life and full of life. Smile and let out a big laugh because regardless of your past, today you can have grace to the brim, bristle, bulge, burst, bustle, buzz, and crawl, hum, overflow, pullulate, and swarm you. Set your expectations high! Enjoy this book and declare over your own life that you are No Longer The Victim!

# Chapter 1

## Who Dropped You?

I know you are probably reading the headline of this chapter wondering if you've ever been dropped. Now understand, I'm not talking about being dropped physically, but rather I'm talking about being dropped mentally, emotionally, or in some other detrimental form. Being dropped is really about things you have encountered that left you injured and wondering how to proceed with life. You must do something about the injury, and the sooner you act the better. Most medical professionals will tell you that people who are seriously injured need immediate attention. The quicker they receive treatment, the more likely they are to make a full recovery. The principle is the same with injuries that cannot be seen—the invisible wounds hidden deep within our hearts. Internal injuries can be just as bad or worse than external injuries. Many people live day after day never getting them treated.

Matters of the soul are serious matters and just like a physical injury, you must rush to the source of help so that the injuries that are only serious don't become fatal. The source I suggest is not a physical place where you meet someone with a lab coat and share your story with them. Maybe you have done that already several times. This place is a secret place that you find all by yourself where you realize that your creator "GOD' wants to be your Daddy and give you the healing that you need. It all starts with you acknowledging that as you look back something did happen.

Many people are pushed into victimhood and eventually reveal that something has been missing in their life for a while. As they sit and reflect they have a hole in their heart that only a fathering could fill. The last prophecy of the Old Testament is a powerful warning about Fathering!

*Behold, I will send you Elijah the prophet before the coming of the great and dreadful day of the Lord: And he shall turn the heart of the fathers to the children, and the heart of the children to their fathers, lest I come and smite the earth with a curse. (Mal. 4:5-6).*

Being a parent of two, I understand a little something about fathering, and you may remember earlier in the book I talked about the loss of my own father. The gist of the verse above is that, "If the spirit of fathering does not come He will curse the earth." The emphasis is the vital role of having a father in your life; and that without a father, many people will find themselves holding a Victims' Club membership.

It's as if life just can't get started for you; and the pain of not having someone afffirm, celebrate, instruct and guide you has caused things to move very slowly for you. Don't feel bad. This book is not to put you down, but instead help you come to terms with the fact that there is life after being dropped. You may be reading and had a great father like I did, but it's still relative to you as well. It's just if you too didn't have a father, or if you don't have one today, you are a part of very unique group of people.

The following are some statistics about fathering in America:

- 85% of all children that exhibit behavioral disorders come from fatherless homes.
- 71% of all high school dropouts come from fatherless homes.
- 75% of all adolescent patients in chemical abuse centers come from fatherless homes.
- 70% of juveniles in state operated institutions come from fatherless homes.
- 85% of all youths sitting in prisons grew up in fatherless homes.
- 80% of rapists motivated with displaced anger come from fatherless homes.
- 90% of all homeless and run away children are from fatherless homes.

These statistics translate to mean that children from a fatherless home are:

- twenty times more likely to have behavioral disorders.
- nine times more likely to drop out of high school.
- ten times more likely to abuse chemical substances.
- nine times more likely to end up in state operated institutions.
- twenty times more likely to end up in prision.
- ten times more likey to commit rape.
- thirty-two times more likely to run away from home.

I am well aware of how statistics are gathered and I know that numbers can be skewed to give many different results and meanings. However, I don't want to overlook such an important subject when we talk about victims. So many people have been dropped by their father and they are sitting on the sideline of life waiting for someone to engage them. I'm telling you with all these facts potentially being true, you don't have to spend the rest of your life as a victim. For many people spend the rest of their lives searching for true love and affirmation, and many never find it.

But that's not how the story ends for the believer, and that's not how your story has to end. When you give your life to Jesus Christ, you become the righteousness of Christ; and in exchange, He gives you a brand new wardrobe called, "His Righteousness." It's simply called being Born Again. When we are Born Again, we become sons and daughters adopted by our Heavenly Father. Wow! Take a minute and celebrate this fundamental shift because it changes everything in your life.

Being born again is like starting over. This is so wonderful because with this new start you get picked up. The same person that was dropped and hurt is now picked up by a loving God who freely gives us a future and hope for tomorrow. He makes us His own and we become His children and He becomes our Daddy.

*For ye have not received the spirit of bondage again to fear; but ye have received the Spirit of adoption, whereby we cry, Abba, Father. The Spirit itself beareth witness with our spirit, that we are the children of God: And if children, then heirs; heirs of God, and joint-heirs with Christ; if so be that we suffer with him, that we may be also glorified together. (Rom. 8:15-17).*

I must warn you that we do have an enemy who wants us to forget the fact that we are the sons and daughters of God. This enemy wants to keep us as bound victims for life. His name is Satan and he fights all that is good and is working with his cohorts to make our lives miserable. He is the hidden agent behind the drop or injury you expereienced and the encounter that left you victimized and hurt. Don't lose your idenity. Remember your legal position in Christ as an heir and joint-heir. Remind yourself daily that you are a child of God and He has a wonderful plan for your life. We've all been hurt before, and sometimes we have to say it out loud. Yes, me too.

**HURT, ABUSE, DIVORCE, REJECTION** – Oh no, not again…

**MISTRUST** – They looked right in my eyes and lied, again.

**SICKNESS** – Where did this come from?  I thought I was healthy.

**FAMILY** – It's one thing when it's problems at work… but home.

**CHILDREN** – I did everything I could for them.

**FINANCES** – I lost my entire life savings in the market crash.

**DEATH OF A LOVED ONE** – Oh no, not my dad…

Don't allow pain to turn you into someone that God has not ordained.  Everyone experiences pain, but you can find life after being a victim. In the Old Testament, there's a story of King David and his covenant with his best friend Jonathan.  Jonathan was the birth son of Saul who was the first king of Israel suceeded by David. One day, David made a promise to Jonathan that he would bless Saul and Jonathan's household if he were to rule as king.  Later, David recalled his promise and sent word throughout Israel that he was looking for someone left from the lineage of Saul. A message was brought back to King David of a young man named Mephibosheth.  Mephibosheth was the crippled son of Jonathan.  When Mephibosheth was five years of age, his father was killed in a great battle.

Mephibosheth's nanny, in the process of fleeing to safety, physically dropped him from her shoulders. As a result of the fall, Mephoisbeth broke both of his legs and was left crippled as a child. At the time of King David's announcement, he was living in a place called Lodabar.

*Saul's son Jonathan had a son named Mephibosheth, who was crippled as a child. He was five years old when the report came from Jezreel that Saul and Jonathan had been killed in battle. When the child's nurse heard the news, she picked him up and fled. But as she hurried away, she dropped him, and he became crippled.*
*(2 Sam. 4:4)*

The name Mephibosheth means shameless. Lodebar was a place of no pasture, dismal, no hope, total desolation. It is very likely that Mephiboseheth could not have visualized life beyond his circumstances. Can you imagine how bad of a situation it was and how painful it must have been for him? The very thought of not being able to use either of your legs and needing someone to help you with every small task gives the feeling of being a victim.

Many people today are suffering as victims. It's not because of their own actions, but like Mephibosheth, someone else dropped them. It's easier to understand falling or tripping, but being dropped by someone else brings a different range of emotions. Some of the same "why questions" asked earlier become relative and many wonder, "Why Me?" Be honest with yourself today and know you are ready to come face to face with whatever or whoever it was that dropped you.

Was it your first husband or wife who dropped you after a wonderful wedding and what looked like a promising future only to discover that something was wrong? You opened up your entire life and trusted them with all of your heart. You tried very hard to make it work and make them happy only to discover that the harder you tried the more you were dropped. After years and years of trying, you moved on; and you still live under a cloud of failure. It's hard and expensive giving love and not getting it back—leaving you with a "why" and many scars.

Was it your mom who dropped you? You always wondered why your mother didn't raise you. Why she may have kept some of the other children, but you were sent to your grandma's house to live. This feeling of major rejection had you asking yourself for years, "Am I good enough?" You may have joined others in trying to work real hard to fit in and be received; but deep down inside, you just wanted to be loved by your birth mother. The pain of being rejected by your own mother is beyond discussion; yet, keeping it bottled up inside, qualifies you as a life time member of the Victims' Club.

Maybe you are a young lady and it's your baby's daddy that dropped you. You never envisioned yourself as a single mom with a child because all you ever wanted was a family. Perhaps when you were a little girl you played on the floor with dolls and looked forward to the day of having a family of your own. Now your reality is that you are all alone and the pain of pregacy and childbirth without a spouse by your side has left you scared and hurt.

Choosing to put a smile on your face and just hide and hold it all in keeps you in the Victims' Club. Maybe you were dropped off in prison to serve a mandatory ten-year sentence. Or maybe you were dropped from finacial insitutions because you filed for bankruptcy ten years ago and you are still in recovery mode. You may suffer from a lack of love and have never had a support system. Maybe you've suffered a broken heart because of the lost of a loved one.

The list goes on and on. For many people reading this, it will cause your thoughts of pain to go a little deeper and remember more dropped moments of pain. That is because you rarely talk about it and you continue to carry the pain of being abused. You were not only dropped but you were dropped off at someone's house whom your parents trusted and you can't tell the rest of the story because it hurts too bad.

I'm not asking you to recall details; but finally, you are at a point where you can release it so that you can move forward. Remember I said earlier that Satan is behind every act of darkness; and his real motive is to completely destroy you and make you a life-long victim. But today he loses and you win! Facing it and receieving God's grace will allow you to relinquish your membership in the Victims' Club.

Here's the good news. Like Mephosibeth, your name is being called; and even with broken limbs, there's royalty in your bloodline. The only thing going for Mephibosheth was his blood line. There was a blessing somewhere in his blood.

He suffered a terrible fall and had two broken legs but something very special was in his blood. Just think about it. The situation looks bad but hope is in the blood. Everyone who saw Mephibosheth only saw his crippled state and his victim status. What they could not see was the blessing of a covanant by right of his bloodline would soon change his physical outcome. Remember you too, have royalty in your bloodline. Eventually the righteousness in you will demand a manifestation. King David searched for Mephibosheth with the intent of "showing him kindness" by asking if there were any remnant of Saul's family that he, David, might show kindness to for his friend Jonathan's sake. (2 Sam. 9:1). Mephibosheth's outcome shifted. The pain of his yesterday was replaced by a future of hope. He would sit at the King's table and be blessed to eat as one of the King's sons. Can you imagine the change in his countenance as he may have said within his own heart, "I was broken, but I'm now blessed!" Yes, somebody dropped me, and it was painful; but today the King has called me to my rightful place at the table, and I've answered his call to be seated with him." This is God's plan for all of us to come to the King's table. The longer you sit at the table, the more the pain will go away and you will be able to bathe in the hope of a glorious future as you sit with the King.

I really believe that when we live our lives in Christ that the joy can far out weigh the pain. You may be wondering like I was, how long did this last and how long was it before Mephibosheth went back to his old life as a victim? But once you taste the goodness that is served at the King's table, who would ever go back?

*But Mephibosheth (who was lame in both feet) moved*
*to Jerusalem to live at the palace*
*(2 Sam. 9:13).*

Your name is being called, and your status is being
changed as you continue to read this book. You never
have to go back to the broken place of victimhood because there will always be a place for you at the King's
table. You are being given the opportunity to eat continually and dwell in the presence of true life and joy.
Accept this invitation and live in the light never looking
back.

As a matter of fact, like Mephibosheth, answer the call,
pack your bags, and move into the palace!

## From Victim To Victor Confession

Father, I thank You today that I will come face to face
with Your life-changing grace. I'm confident in knowing that when I come face to face with You, Oh God,
Your unmerited grace will call me into being everything
that You have ordained for my life.

I declare and decree today that I am stronger and focused on the assignment you have given me. For You,
Oh Lord, are my sun and shield, granting grace and
glory always. For there is no good thing that You will
withhold from me as I focus on walking upright in You.
(Ps. 84:11). I pause today to celebrate the grace of God
in my life, and I am the recipient of perfect strength.

# Chapter 2

## One-On-One with Grace

Are you ready for a one-on-one encounter with Grace? In the previous chapter we learned what Mephibosheth experienced was God's grace. You see, God's grace repairs us and empowers us to live and love again. God's designed grace is so powerful, but yet it won't overtake or overwhelm us. It is so very personal that it requires each of us to have a personal encounter with Him. Get ready to burst at the seams and be filled with grace until you become extremely thankful for everything in your life. Begin a life of praise and worship that's so incredible and receive supernatural enablement everyday.

Be mindful and take notice because when you should be worn out, and tired you will feel fresh and replenished for the grace of God is at work in your life. This grace that's operating within you will make you feel clean and refreshed that hopefully you will no longer feel like a victim or an orphan.

This grace will come to you in two very distinct ways—
saving and enabling.

## Saving Grace

Saving Grace is the grace you received when you ac-
cepted salvation and the blessings of what the Cross
provided for you. Jesus Christ died on the cross for
our sins and has paid the price in full for us to have
eternal life with the Father forever. This saving grace
prepares us for so much more.

## Enabling Grace

We are saved by saving grace, but enabling grace supplies the ability to live Christ honoring lives. This enabling grace also empowers us to follow the Holy Spirit
and to hear God speaking to us. Enabling grace helps
us to fulfill our various callings and honor Christ with
our lives.

You may have looked at your life experiences and because of what you've been through, never saw yourself
being free, blessed, and flourishing. Grace empowers
you to be something you've never imagined being on
your own! This grace begins to peel off the pain of the
past and the transparent you comes forth. You should
like the new and empowered you.

When you felt like a victim you were trapped in fear and
darkness. So many things muddled your true identity.
But when true grace comes into your life it brings affirmation and identity so that the transparent you, the
new and improved you can shine forth. As you grow
in grace you should no longer see yourself helpless or
hopeless.

This personal grace encounter gives you power to now conquer what you previously only dared to do. Grace is divine enablement. It is God's anointing given to you so that you can be empowered to fulfill your God given assignments.

Remember when you were in darkness and feeling like a victim it became harder and harder with every growing day. Now that you are experiencing God's Grace you will grow into new measures of grace everyday and see your life taking new shapes and colors as you grow. The Apostle Paul makes a powerful statement about grace when he said, *"I am that I am by the grace of God and His grace which was bestowed upon me was not in vain . . . but the grace of God which was with me. (1 Cor. 15:10).*

This means, that with grace I'm now made into someone I never imagined I could be. Wow! So many people spend so much time looking, comparing, and measuring themselves against others. But grace empowers me to be unique so that I can be released to be me. I can now settle into the new reality of not being like anyone and focus all my attention on becoming like Christ. Now I can claim the whole great truth that teaches me that the best use of life is striving to be like the One who set me free. Speaking of freedom, when I break away from being a victim and receive God's grace, I also realize that he freed me from so much more. He set me free so I could become like Him. That's why I could not remain a victim because my Heavenly Father wants me to be like Him and I could never do that bound. Don't think that this new freedom is about you and remain there stuck in that place.

It's a far bigger picture than you. Just thinking it's all about you will cause you to return back to the Victims' Club. With this new freedom, you and I must grab hold of a larger vision that says your new life is about Him and not you. Reflect but don't look back on where you were and the pain you were in. Remember, He called your name like David called Mephosibeth, and He showed you kindness and grace. For to me to live is Christ. . . (Phil. 1:21)

True, Grace basically says that when man was helpless and could do nothing about his condition, God sent His Son to die. Grace teaches us that God has supplied a power and force that gets us through our greatest pain and worst injury in life. It's hard to be a victim ever again because the grace of God supernaturally enables us with an ability and power to live and enjoy life without cracking, falling, or folding.

This kind of strength is called the Sufficiency of Grace. Remember, I told you earlier that at one of my lowest moments I received an answer from the Lord that His grace was sufficient for me. But what really is the sufficiency of Grace?

• Grace is adequate enough; meaning it's for anything.

• Grace is God's strength replacing our weaknesses.

• Grace brings us into the glory of God.

Have you ever wondered why so many people who claim to know God have contradictory testimonies? One day they were lost, hurt, broken victims.

The Lord gave them grace and rescued them from a life of pain. They were able to get up out of their pain and make progress only to return back to their former lives. They seem to use the Lord as an emergency 911 service to only call Him when they are in trouble—only to walk away from Him after they are rescued. That is not God's plan for us. He does not want us to have a seasonal relationship and fellowship with Him. God loves us so much that He allows certain things in our lives to keep us under His grace. The Apostle Paul talks about a thorn being in his flesh. It is this thorn that seemed to keep him on his knees. Paul is living with his own combination of pain and prayer. God's plan is to keep us inside of His grace. His desire is that we never forget our true purpose to walk with Him everyday. He knows exactly what we need; and thankfully He allows reminders, reflection, and repeated courses.

The Apostle Paul's thorn was so painful that I can envision his tears mixed with his prayer, Three different times I begged the Lord to take it away (2 Cor. 12:8). I'm so glad that verses like this exist in the Bible for our understanding. God allows us to see behind the scenes of those who lived in biblical days. Verses like this are so helpful in identifying with the Apostle Paul that I can shout a loud declaration of "Me too." Let's take a moment and think about how people feel at times praying to God that He would take something out of their lives that they really want gone. The verse says that Paul prayed three times asking God to take the thorn away. Obviously it was something that was really troubling him.

This brings us to the point now where we really dig into the heart of feeling like a victim because times like these are when we are cast down to such a low place that we feel hopeless and helpless. As Christians we reach out to God knowing that He will help us, yet we've already made the mistake of premeditation in our thinking the best way for Him to help us. Instead of us praying and simply asking the Lord for help, we ask Him to remove the thorn like Paul. The Lord knows what's best for us, and He may not remove the thorn, but instead do something better—bring us face-to-face with His grace.

If we are not careful during these times of great pain and loss, the enemy will really play mental trickery with our minds causing us to revert back to being a victim and feeling low and hopeless. We must accept all our challenges and problems as new opportunities for the Lord to show us a new dimension of His love that we have yet to know. I recently had this exact experience in my life where I asked the Lord the exact same thing, "Remove this thorn." His response was similar to that given to the Apostle Paul and it was, "Grace" or in my case, "Grace, Grace." For a short time I felt hopeless and helpless like any victim would. I've come to understand that emotion was needed so I could experience the Grace encounter. I toiled and wrestled until finally I looked up and asked the Lord, 'Why'? How many times have you either asked God or thought to ask God, "Why me?" Join the ranks of so many that have asked that question over and over again. This book is about taking you from asking the question, "Why Me?" to asking the question, "Why not me?" and finally making the statement, "I'm glad it's me!"

Join the ranks of so many that have asked that question over and over again. This book is about taking you from asking the question, "Why Me?" to asking the question, "Why not me?" and finally making the statement, "I'm glad it's me!" Yes, I am glad it was me in this situation, and I am so glad today that the Lord chose me for this one-on-one encounter with His grace so that I could grow and expand in my knowledge of Him.

To really be delivered from being a victim, you must see every event as an opportunity to grow and expand your vision for life. Initially, if so, painful; but through faith you can turn it into power and use it as a leaping pad. The very reason we are in the challenge might be a surprise. The Bible later reveals to us why Paul had this thorn.

*And lest I should be exalted above measure through the abundance of the revelations, there was given to me a thorn in the flesh, the messenger of Satan to buffet me, lest I should be exalted above measure, (2 Cor. 12:7).*

What was really at stake here was Paul being lifted up too high because of the abundance of revelation he received. God loved him so much that He allowed this thorn to keep Paul humbled and balanced. Look at how committed the Heavenly Father is in keeping us under the covering of His grace.

## You never want to get too high and outside of grace.

Grace is depending on God and trusting Him. The opposite of grace is our strength and flesh. At our lowest moment when we are feeling like a victim, God's grace will come in and rest upon us.

We don't have to use our strength to make anything happen. As I rely and depend upon Him daily, I realize that the current challenge could be the very thing that is keeping me from being exalted above measure. Historically, man has been known to sometimes get a little too high and inflated in self. We need a recollection of what life is really about. For believers, it's about bringing honor to the Heavenly Father and serving others. So during the trial or test, we can't let all of our focus be on ourselves but on remembering that we have a larger vision.

Another part of a victim mentality is when you can only look at yourself, and in looking at yourself you see yourself, too weak to reach out and help others. Again, I stress the importance of having this one-on-one intimate encounter with Grace because it will bring healing and rid you of the victim mentality. As you move forward in this encounter you will soon discover that grace is God's power replacing your weaknesses. This is the healthy part of shedding off the victim syndrome when Grace meets you in the middle of your crisis that's causing such weakness and reveals to you a pathway forward. Now you are in a time of discovery, and you can receive real answers for your future. You will grow and develop and be a stronger person because you have come face to face with Grace.

# Regardless of Your Questions, Get Ready for God's Answer.

*Each time He said. "My grace is all you need. My power works best in weakness." So now I am glad to boast about my weaknesses, so that the power of Christ can work through me.*
*(2 Cor 12:9).*

Don't you just love real answers from our Heavenly Father! Paul, who might have been feeling like a victim himself, received a long awaited answer to his prayer. It's not the answer he asked for. Remember he asked for the thorn to be taken away. Maybe there's been a time in your moments of reflection on your life where you might have said, "I wish that never happened," and that's perfectly fine. Your reality is that it did happen, and you need Grace to overcome it. It might still be happening but you need Grace and strength to make it day to day. The answer that Apostle Paul received is your answer and mine as well. However, it is somewhat complex but must be fully embraced. It will hopefully cause you to have an epiphany. God says four important things in this one verse:

- My Grace is all you need.
- My power works best in weakness.
- Most gladly therefore will I rather glory in my infirmities.
- The power of Christ may rest upon me

This is good news for everyone who has ever felt like a victim. Now you are on a new road of recovery and I again welcome you to the world of Sufficient Grace.

Something is very special about this statement. If you allow it to soak deep within, you will discover that the word sufficient is a key ingredient.

Webster identifies sufficient as an adjective, and defines it as having or providing as much as is needed. He is sufficient for me. His sufficiency is the exact amount of pre-measured help that I need for my thorn. Whatever happened that made me feel like a victim has held me for a while, but today I embrace the sufficiency of Grace. It's just what you and I need. It's there every time I need it so I'm never alone and I'm always covered by it. This grace holds me and repairs me. It doesn't allow me to remain bound by the old chains of abuse, fear, inadequacy, torment, rejection, and pain. I've found the grace of God for me personally and I won't ever let it go.

Then He leads me further by teaching me that when this "Sufficient Grace" comes into my life and I receive it, new strength comes along with it. This is the same strength that comes to those who've been weakened by something or someone. I like to call it perfect strength at the perfect time. According to this verse, we have strength from above available, made perfect in times of weakness. Believe me when I tell you that no one is going to understand this phenomenon so don't waste precious time trying to explain it because its your personal encounter. Remember that this chapter is called one-on-one with grace. It's from this experience that your new mind-set is shaped. Make these confessions and continue to bathe yourself in His amazing grace.

# From Victim to Victor Confession

GRACE IS – God's sufficiency in every aspect
      of my life.
GRACE IS – Perfect strength in the face of human
      weakness.
GRACE IS – The glory of God and giving glory
      to glory in the middle of it.
GRACE IS – The power of the Lord Jesus Christ
      coming to rest on my life like a mantle.

Now that you have come face-to-face with Grace you should sense the shift. You should feel stronger and extremely excited about your future because perfect strength has taken over you now. When you were feeling like a victim you felt so weak and so worn out. Now you have joy and are able to be excited about a new tomorrow.

What do you think happens next? Your attitude begins to change. Notice what Apostle Paul says next, "Most gladly therefore will I rather glory in my infirmity." What a major switch in his attitude.

The attitude change that comes from feeling helpless, to seeing, saying, and looking at the problem differently. You must find a way to be joyful and thankful even though the problem is not resolved yet. Most people who have felt like they were victims sit back and wait until their situation gets better and then they have a better attitude. But this kind of grace calls for us to praise God at all times, being thankful even though we are still dealing with unresolved issues.

This healthy approach sends a signal to everything and everyone around you that your season is changing. It's taking down the surrender flag and raising your Nissi battle flag so that even your opponent knows that a new fight has been stirred up on the inside of you. Finally, this verse says that as a result of my attitude change, "the power of Christ may rest upon me." It's getting better and stronger everyday all the while the power of the Lord Jesus Christ comes and rests upon me. Now you may ask, "Where was this power when I was suffering as a victim?" "Where was this power in my recovery?" "Where was this power when I felt rejected and alone?" This power was there all of the time, knocking at your door. You just never answered the door. Instead, your fears and discouragement would answer the door and the power was not invited in. Now that you are walking in strength and you have changed your perspective, this power can come and rest on your shoulders and guide your life. Be very careful. In order to sustain this powerful position in life, you will need to have continual time for prayer, worship, and studying of God's word.

This power is not just released one time on one day, but it is a continual flow that you receive as you live obediently and remain in a posture of humility. Commit these verses to memory just in case the coldness of victimhood tries to return. You may go through various trials, but now you know you can always run quickly to the dressing room of grace and quickly be supplied with supernatural strength. It works during any type of trial. On five different occasions, Apostle Paul shows us that grace allows us to be thankful and focused;

*Therefore I take pleasure in infirmities, in reproaches, in necessities, in persecutions, in distresses for Christ's sake. . .(2 Cor. 12:10).*

We are completely covered when we are under God's grace and whatever is thrown at us—infirmities, reproaches, necessities, persecutions or distresses—grace out powers them all. We have the constant supply from our Heavenly Father to press through it because of our encounter with grace.

# Chapter 3

## No Longer the Victim

It is necessary to really understand what a victim is. It is a mentality; an acquired, learned personality trait in which a person tends to regard him or herself as a victim of negative actions from others and to think, speak and act based on those actions. Victims produce a relatively high frequency of negative emotional states such as anger, sadness, and or fear. Many victims are addicted to the sympathy of it all. A victim's mentality may manifest itself in a range of different behaviors or ways of thinking and talking. Let's take a look at how it manifests itself within.

- Blaming others for a situation that one has created or significantly contributed to. Failing or unwilling to take responsibility for one's own actions or the actions to which one has contributed.

- The Why Me Syndrome - Believing that other people are generally or fundamentally luckier and happier than you. "Why me, Lord?"

- Gaining short-term pleasure from feeling sorry for oneself or eliciting pity from others.

- Get sympathy and feel better when telling exaggerated stories about bad deeds of other people, especially during gossip.

- Extremely negative with general tendency to focus on bad rather than good aspects of a situation. A glass that is half full is considered half empty.

- Defensive in conversation. Always reading a non-existent negative intention into a neutral question and reacting with a corresponding accusation which hinders the collective solution of problems and instead creates unnecessary conflict.

- Unadventurous and generally unwilling to take risks. Habitually exaggerates the importance or likelihood of possible negative outcomes.

- Exhibiting learned helplessness and underestimating one's ability or influence in a given situation—often left feeling powerless.

- Stubborn all the while tending to reject suggestions or constructive criticism from others who listen and care; unable. Reluctant to implement suggestions of others for one's own benefit.

- Self-deprecating and putting oneself down even further than others are supposedly doing.

Once again, I ask you to not take this personal. Victims carry an aroma that people can smell and detect. Victims also hang out together and share how bad their pain is individually and collectively. Darkness looks for people who are victims because they are easy prey.

It's time for a paradigm shift. It's time for a radical shift in your thinking so that you begin to see yourself as a winner and not a whiner. The language may seem very strong, but you're ready for a mind shift because you are ready to win. As you look back over your life you have spent time whining consumed with pity and sorrow. But today you are ready to rise up. Congratulations! Let me be the first to celebrate you and declare that you are, "No Longer A Victim." After coming face-to-face you should be ready to declare with me that you are no longer the victim. As a matter of fact, the Apostle Paul teaches us a powerful principle about strength: *... for when I am weak, then am I strong. (2 Cor. 12:10).*

You can see from this verse that how you view yourself and what you say to yourself is one of the major key principles in life. Paul says that even though he may be weakened that he is yet strengthened. That may seem impossible to you but you are living supernaturally now. So declare with me that in spite of your weaknesses yet you are strong. This gives you a healthy self-image. You begin to see yourself as someone who is strong and not weak. Soon you will notice that as you embrace this victorious posture that you will live every day of your life on purpose and without apology.

Maybe you're the person who spends a lot of time encouraging others and reminding them of their worth. It is okay to take a short breath and remind yourself of what you can be.

Recently, I sat on an airplane and learned a very powerful lesson. Before we took off, the pilot asked that we stop whatever we were doing and watch the instructional video that contained vital safety information. As I watched the video, the voice of the speaker made it very clear, "If the cabin loses pressure, a mask will drop from above your head. Place the mask on yourself first. If you are sitting next to a child or older person assist them with their mask second."

This was a very important lesson for me. I always thought you should help others before you help yourself. In some cases this may be true. But in the case of the airplane message, how can you help others to breathe when you are running out of air for yourself? It's the same way with seeing yourself whole and complete. It positions you with a greater capacity to assist others.

Practice everyday saying, "I am strong; I have purpose in my life; I will not be defeated by my pain; I have capacity to give." The more you seek to give, the better your life will become. Victims aren't able to give anything. This is a great way to measure where you are in life. If you find that you do a great job at receiving, and watching others give but a poor job at giving, you might be a victim. Giving is a sign of strength and might. It helps you transition to the good part of life. Do not be a life-long receiver and miss out on the joy of giving. Remember, you are no longer the victim.

Even if you have been burned in the past, use wisdom before you open up your heart and give away all of the riches that is within you. A smile, a hug, a kind word, it's all giving; and you have what it takes to do it. Relax, reflect, and release to others from the place of strength that you are now called to walk in.

So if it's true that you are no longer a victim, then we need to find a new title and a new description for who you are going to be. Let's consider the word *victor*. New Oxford American Dictionary defines *victor* as a person who defeats an enemy or opponent in a battle, game, or other competition. *Victor* is the root word in the word *Victory* and should make you feel like your true self.

You are a victor. The new and improved you is now being revealed to the world today. Those who had written you off as a life-long victim might be in for a little surprise. A victor is someone who is winning. As long as you are striving you are winning. Some people determine winners by the final score. Others determine winners by how the game is played. I want to describe a winner as someone who plays the game and never quits. As long as you are striving, you are winning. As long as you keep winning, you will keep striving. Can you imagine how your friends are going to view you now? Can you imagine how different life is going to be as a victor? Can you imagine how powerful your testimony and story will be now that you are a victor? As a victim you were limited and lacking, but now through grace you are connected to God who has unlimited power and resources to pour out into your life.

One day I was talking to my family about being victors. We decided that everyone in the family would get a Bible verse that they could memorize and quote it everyday on our way to becoming victors. This is the verse I chose:

*Now thanks be unto God, which always causeth us to triumph in Christ, and maketh manifest the savour of his knowledge by us in every place.*
*(2 Cor. 2:14).*

I chose this verse because it gave me such a sense of empowerment. This verse says that God always causes us to triumph. New Oxford American defines triumph as "being victorious or successful; winning; receiving honors upon return from a victory."

This is where I get excited! I hope the same excitement exists within you. You see not only are we victors but we are called to triumph. Just look at how far you've come and how powerful Grace is. One day you can be sitting down feeling sorry for yourself and the next day you're walking in victory. Not the kind of victory that you have to hide and apologize for but public victory that can be described as triumph. Triumph goes beyond winning and takes us to a front row seat at the victory party. To triumph means to celebrate the victory and look back and rejoice over the accomplishments. In ancient Rome, when the commanders returned from a victorious battle, they were not allowed to return home quietly. The people would prepare for "triumph" and have a public celebration of the commander and the army who'd just won the battle. This public celebratory display and affirmation released a positive energy and served as a source of encouragement for more good works. Everyone needs to be celebrated. Today I give you permission to stop and celebrate yourself as a victor and a person who has been called to triumph. I caution you however, that you may catch a few eyes from people around you that may not understand what's going on with you. It's all okay. They most likely weren't around when you were in your low place, so they didn't see you during your time of struggle. Walk in humility and stay connected to friends you love. Don't allow their misunderstanding of the new you to stop you from celebrating. Your journey has been too long and you have fought too hard. Your victory is worth more than a sneak back into town. Come back like the commanders from ancient rome—pageantry and circumstance—await your great triumph arrival. As you walk in triumph, you will walk into a new season in life and many new doors will open for you. Be cautious, for often times opposition may try to sneak into the new doors but don't be discouraged. You are still a victor.

*For a great door and effectual is opened unto me, and there are many adversaries (1 Cor. 16:9).*

This is an important warning because as long as you continue to walk in victory, something will always try to pull you back to being a victim. Many times when opposition comes, it tries to pull you back to the other times in your life when you felt opposed and broken. Don't allow this to happen. Remain strong and focus on the big picture, which is "triumph." Strive through grace to see things differently and know that many times adversaries are a sign of the open door. This is the season of open doors. God is redeeming time for you so keep the momentum going.

Many people come in contact with opposition and stop as if they've hit a brick wall. When you face opposition, keep walking. Walk through it and never stop for one moment to feel helpless. Confess in the midst of opposition. "I am strong; I am mighty; I am complete; I am healed; I am whole; I am becoming." You are becoming what God has in mind for you when He first created you. Don't allow new challenges to shatter your new-found confidence. Remember to keep seeing yourself as your Father sees you. Listen and hear the sound of the victory music playing for you as you triumph and keep moving so that you remain strong and firm in your new walk of victory. Let me suggest the principle of consecration and concentration.

## Consecration

*And Joshua said unto the people, sanctify yourselves: for tomorrow the Lord will do wonders among you. (Josh. 3:5).*

## Concentration

*Wherefore seeing we also are compassed about with so great a cloud of witnesses, let us lay aside every weight, and the sin which doth so easily beset us, and let us run with patience the race that is set before us. Looking unto Jesus the author and finisher of our faith; who for the joy that was set before him endured the cross, despising the shame, and is set down at the right hand of the throne of God. (Heb. 12:1-2).*

Let me be the first to congratulate you and celebrate you because you are graduating from the Victim Assistance Program. You are being weaned off and weaned on. As you are weaned away from co-dependence, you are introduced and weaned on to the grace of God. Something in you will shift. The Holy Spirit is going to continually feel strong on the inside of you. Get ready for your tears to be replaced with joy and for grace and order to move within you. Get ready to live the rest of your life as a victor.

## From Victim To Victor Confession

Today, I declare that I am no longer a victim and decree I am a victor. I acknowledge that I've been hurt, but today I receive the grace of God for all of my pain. God's grace is my strength that is made perfect in my weakness and He is there for me. With Him, "I have strength like no other." Today I declare that I will not allow the feelings and emotions of the past to rob me of my grace future in Christ Jesus. In Christ Jesus I am victorious! I am not moved by overwhelming feelings or past failures because God is bigger and more powerful than anything and everything I've ever been through. I walk in the promises God has for me and His Word transforms my mind. No matter what my situation looks like, I choose to believe God's truth and tear down the devil's lies. I am not defeated! I have set my hope in Jesus and by faith I walk in victory. From this day forward I declare the Word of God over my Life.

# Chapter 4

## Grace Looks Good On You

From the moment you embrace your new identity in Christ, it changes the way you look. Being a victim carries contention and a posture of defeat. When you shed this posture and receive the grace to move forward, your look begins to change. You are now on your way to being excited about your future. The favor on your life actually makes you look brighter. God is light. Those connected to Him carry a light that cannot hide from any problem or circumstance. As your newfound liberty begins to manifest, you are experiencing life as God has ordained it. You were not created to be broken, but you were created in the image and likeness of God. God created you for something special and according to the book of Genesis, you and I were created to bring glory back to God. When we live our lives to His honor, others are able to see that we are connected to Him and as a result He is pleased. The Bible is very clear that God created us to be powerful; but the god of this world, Satan, is working as hard as he can to keep people powerless.

The word **world** comes from the word *cosmos*, having to do with the order or arrangement of things.

You see, our enemy is Satan. He stole the authority of the world from Adam when Adam disobeyed the instructions of God. The reason we have pain and suffering is because we live in a fallen world. Maybe you have wondered like I have, "Why do bad things happen to good people?" "Why do we have to go through certain things?" "Why did this happen to me?" The answer is sin. We live in a fallen world. The enemy brought chaos into the world, and it lead to the state of the world that we witness today. Somebody may say, "Well, it looks pretty orderly to me." The order is being established through the coming of God's kingdom. However, when you look at the world system, you see lawlessness and injustice, poverty and sickness, disease and premature death, disasters and despair, toiling and sweating trying to make ends meet, demonic forces and dominions, hatred and jealously, racism and deception.

Maybe now you understand why we needed to be rescued by God's grace. How powerful a rescue it is when God brings us out. Many people are controlled by these influences. They commit acts led by darkness that hurt the person the act is committed against, leaving them mad and in the state of being a victim. If you are going to wear grace and continue to allow it to look good on you, you must develop the discipline of watching. Everyday something is trying to trap you and snare you so that you can fall back into the pit and lose your grace-flow.

You must be sober and watchful. The Bible says that as the wicked one prowls around, he is looking to trap a particular type of person. For the Bible tells us to be careful. Watch out for attacks from Satan, your great enemy, because he prowls around like a hungry, roaring lion, looking for some victim to tear apart (1 Pet. 5:8).

This should really get your attention that Satan is looking for someone who is a victim because he knows in most cases they are weakened and unsupported. This is why you must wear the clothing of grace. When the enemy sees that you're clothed in grace, he moves on. But when the devil sees those who are not clothed in grace, those who are hurt and rejected, he makes an attempt to deceive them with lies into greater darkness. You have to make a decision whether to be a victim or a victor. The quicker you decide, the quicker you can resist his darkness. You can't be both victim and victor. The decision of victor allows for wearing the garment of grace like a new wardrobe. Victors don't allow the enemy to pull them back into darkness. Instead, they move forward into the light of Jesus Christ. As you press forward, keep in mind that Jesus has already prepared a seat for you with Him in heavenly places.

*But God, who is rich in mercy, for His great love wherewith He loved us, Even when we were dead in sins, hath quickened us together with Christ, (by grace ye are saved;) And hath raised us up together, and made us sit together in heavenly places in Christ Jesus. In the ages to come, He might show the exceeding riches of his grace in his kindness toward us through Christ Jesus.* (Eph. 2:4-7).

This is a special seat and unique kindness that we receive as members of God's family. You can't take this seat wearing your old attitude and disposition. You cannot sit with the resurrected Lord in heavenly places and still cling to your victim status. It is because of His crucifixion that we are crucified; because of His death that we must die daily; because of His descension that we must descend; because of His resurrection that we are risen; and because He sits at the right hand, that we then are seated with Him. You must realize that whatever they put on you was already placed on Him. Everything they did or are trying to do was put on Him; therefore, you no longer need to carry it. The Apostle Peter makes it clear that Christ carried our sins for us, *"Who his own self bare our sins in his own body on the tree, that we, being dead to sins, should live unto righteousness: by whose stripes ye were healed"* (2 Pet. 2:24).

The New Living Translation allows us to see this scripture from a personal understanding;

"He personally carried our sins in His body on the cross so that we can be dead to sin and live for what is right. By His wounds you were healed."

This seat calls for you to wear grace. So put it on now and take your new position in Him as an act of God's unmerited favor. Make these confessions everyday and allow yourself to be filled with new energy and discovery.

- I am a winner because I am completely dependent on God for strength in order to resist the things that would make me less than a winner.

- I am a winner because I have Christ-confidence; He gives me faith to place absolute trust in His words, which are the only reliable authority.

- I am a winner because I am made in the image and likeness of my Creator, Who gave me a burning desire, a measure of talent and faith to attempt the difficult and overcome the seemingly impossible. To see defeat as temporary, as a chance to fight that battle better next time and gain an even greater victory as a result of what I've learned.

Many times in my own life I've had to remind myself of such confessions. Positive faith statements can keep us in a God-ward posture and receiving God's best for us. It's all about having a positive attitude and when you have a victorious one, "Grace Looks Good on You." Your vision has now expanded allowing you to see things differently. You see process and progress. You might not be there yet, and you may still have a long way to go, but your self-image is now healthy. You're beginning to follow God's blueprint for your life.

Dr. Martin Luther King, Jr. once said to a group of high school students, "What Is Your Life's Blueprint?" *"And when you discover what you will be in your life, set out to do it as if God Almighty called you at this particular moment in history to do it. Don't just set out to do a good job. Set out to do such a good job that the living, the dead or the unborn couldn't do it any better.*

*If it falls your lot to be a street sweeper, sweep streets like Michelangelo painted pictures, sweep streets like Beethoven composed music, sweep streets like Leontyne Price sings before the Metropolitan Opera. Sweep streets like Shakespeare wrote poetry. Sweep streets so well that all the hosts of heaven and earth will have to pause and say: Here lived a great street sweeper who swept his job well....*

*For it isn't by size that you win or fail. Be the best of whatever you are."*

Victors see their own possibilities and strive to be the biggest shrub. As you continue on this path, more and more change will come into you life.

I'd like to invite you to take a journey with me to what I call the Dressing Room of Grace. I'm sure you have heard stories of people getting makeovers and how the end result was so wonderful. This is what God wants to do for you. This is why your journey has been so hard. The bigger the assignment, the harder the journey because it is where the beauty that's within is manifested externally. We have talked about grace long enough for it to soak deep inside but you can't keep it all to yourself. Someone needs to hear your story. Your testimony is power-packed with real life changing potency that will bless others.

Several months ago I had a vision of the Lord taking me into a very large dressing room. Everything was exceptionally beautiful as I stood there waiting to see what would happen next. As I stood in the vision, the Father started speaking about what He wanted to dress me in. He explained that when you are healed from your heaviness, He gives you new garments. These new garments represent garments of praise for the spirit of heaviness. It is here in the dressing room where the Father will give you, peace, joy, righteousness, honor, love, wholeness, might, strength, prosperity, glory, power, confidence and grace.

## From Victim To Victor Confession

### Confess this verse over your life:
*"Now the Lord is that Spirit: and where the Spirit of the Lord is, there is liberty. But we all, with open face beholding as in a glass the glory of the Lord, are changed into the same image from glory to glory, even as by the Spirit of the Lord." (2 Corinthians 3:17-18, KJV).*

# Chapter 5

## Finally, Confident!

There are many Scriptures in the Bible that remind us the Lord is our confidence and that He will keep us from being taken over by the enemy (Prov. 3:26). This is particularly important to remember because at times our confidence can be broken by life's circumstances. An excellent example of a confidence-breaker in the Bible happened at a well. One day Jesus insisted to His disciples that He would have to pass through a territory that in the grand scheme was not necessary to enter. It was a town called Samaria where He encountered a woman who had been stripped of her confidence by society. His words to her that really hit her heart were, "Go and get your husband." It was a statement that ripped at her confidence. Her embarrassing response was, "I don't have a husband." And Jesus agreed, stating, "You're right, you have no husband" (John 4:4-17). Similar modern day statements rip our confidence to pieces.

Modern day statements such as: How is your mother doing? Are you still working? How's your daughter's condition? Do you still live there? Have you heard from your dad? How was the funeral? What did the doctor say? Are you still getting married? Do you still go to church? Did you lose your job? Is money tight? Where's your husband?

At some point we have to get down to the real issue and source of pain. No one and nothing has permission any more to keep you from being confident. Hopefully, you have been led down a path where you have found your voice and your confidence is growing. Contrary to popular belief, you don't ever have to be content or confined in situations that shatter your confidence. Many people are shy because of their confidence, and they wear the label of an introvert. An introvert is someone who is reserved and shy. Many times the shyness is because of a lack of confidence. Introverts are drained by social encounters and energized by solitary creative pursuits. Their disposition is frequently misconstrued as shyness, social phobia, or even personality disorder. So many factors contribute to a lack of confidence. Remember, you can never defeat a problem that you don't understand. Thank God that regardless of all that you've been through, you can still be a person of confidence. As I discussed earlier, the real culprit is Satan. He works behind the scenes using the voices of others and even your own mind to make you feel low and lack confidence. He will try to use;

Your size--height or lack of height
Your family structure--dysfunctional or incomplete
Your accomplishments---good or bad
Your education---or lack there of
Your financial success or financial failures
Your broken homes or broken relationships
Your Lack---of love or affirmation
Your loneliness and rejection...or
Your anything.

It's important that you remember that Satan's entire purpose is to continually combat us with negativity—forever reminding us of our weaknesses and what we don't do very well. Our confidence is developed and strengthened through prayer, worship, study, and confession of the Word of God. We must hold fast to this confidence...through Christ Jesus. In the book of Hebrews, the Apostle Paul tells us to, "Cast not away therefore your confidence which hath great recompense of reward. For ye have need of patience, that after you have done the will of God, ye might receive the promise" (Hebrews 10:34-36). Many people get right to the doorway of their victory and a challenge comes which causes them to give up. Reflecting on how far you've come can be helpful. When you see the long road behind you, it should help you buckle down and get a tighter grip on confidence. "Though a host should encamp against you, your heart shall not fear; though war should rise against thee, in this be confident" (Psalms 27:1-3).

# FOCUS, VISION AND CONCENTRATION

Every day when you wake—focus. Give your complete, undivided with an intense mental engrossment, immersed, and absorbed attention to Christ. Focus requires your faculties and mental concentration to come into alignment with and keeping track of all the details required for complete attention. There are no distractions when you are focused. Focus is connected to confidence. Now let me warn you, before we go any further, that I'm not talking about self-confidence. The kind of confidence I am talking about is the confidence that lives deep down inside of you as a result of a life that is submitted in total obedience to the Lord. David reminds us that, *"Blessed is the man who does not walk not in the counsel of the wicked, nor stand in the seat of mockers. But his delight is in the law of the Lord, and on his law he meditates day and night. He is like a tree planted by the streams of water which yields its fruit in season and whose leaf does not wither. Whatever he does shall prosper"* (Psalms 1).

Remember, it is not self-confidence but rather it is God working in you through His Son. It's the kind of confidence that reminds you daily that you are a work under construction. "Being confident of this very thing, that He who hath begun a good works in you will perform it until the day of Jesus Christ" (Phil. 1:6). You are headed towards greatness. Step-by-step, your confidence should be growing. Don't let a lack of confidence become a habit for you. A habit is something you continually do without thinking about it.

Allow the word of God to continually wash your mind and bring you into the type of grace that releases confidence in you.

The question now becomes very direct and simple. It is simple in the sense that if you are able to define and focus on who started you on your journey, then you will have full assurance and confidence about your direction. The Bible says we can be confident about God completing what he starts. We know that our Heavenly Father completes what He begins. We can be confident in His abilities and willingness to complete what He has started in our lives. If your life is a combination of self-led projects, then you can't share in this confidence. But, on the contrary, if the Lord is directing your life, and if He has started you on this journey of faith, then surely He will complete and mature His purpose in you. This should give you great confidence.

To maintain your confidence, don't spend too much time looking at yourself or measuring your gifts. A better use of life is to turn your attention to serving those around you—discovering and being led in new ways you can make a difference. By focusing on yourself you notice flaws that tear away at your self-confidence, which is not the kind of confidence that you've been given through grace.

Remember that the confidence we have flows out of our relationship with the Lord. In the Bible it appears that Moses really struggled with his inability to speak well and it tore away at his confidence;

*"But Moses pleaded with the Lord, 'O Lord, I'm not very good with words. I never have been, and I'm not now, even though you have spoken to me. I get tongue-tied, and my words get tangled.' Then the Lord asked Moses, 'Who makes a person's mouth? Who decides whether people speak or do not speak, hear or do not hear, see or do not see? Is it not I, the Lord? Lord'"*
(Exod. 4:10-11 NLT).

God knows everything about you. He has filled you with His Spirit. He wants you to be confident in Him. It's easy to spend time constantly focusing on what's wrong with you. All that does is shatters your confidence even the more. Many people subconsciously see themselves as victims because all their lives they've focused on the disappointments and negative factors. Moses was so consumed by his inadequacies that he could not move forward. Even when God gave him an assignment, Moses buckled and complained that he could not fulfill the assignment because of his stuttered speech. Remember God is omniscient; He knows every little detail about you. To walk in confidence, you have to shift your focus from what you can't do to what you can do.

In 2013, after the death of my father, I decided that I would stop spending so much time focusing on problems and instead shift my focus to solutions and possibilities. No one does everything well, and no one person has been given everything. I believe that everyone is born with a special set of gifts and abilities that they can do well. When those gifts are developed and enhanced they will help increase the quality of lives for those around you and ultimately improve your life. Now you should be ready to declare that you are fearfully and wonderfully made.

King David reminds us that we are fearfully and wonderfully made and marvelous are His works and our inner soul knows right well (Ps. 139:14).

Yes, God made you for something special. This book has been about being able to discover what that special purpose is. When a person sees himself or herself as a victim, they are technically in shutdown mode and not discovery mode. I often times had to remind myself over and over again that I'm fearfully and wonderfully made. God has given me His Grace to personally empower me to live victoriously. Grace in its simplicity is God's unmerited, undeserved, and unearned favor. It seems so simple to human reasoning, yet it is so much more powerful than our fleshly understanding. To walk in confidence you must allow God's pure grace to soak deeply within you.

This grace is God's supernatural characteristic that rains down on us empowering and enabling us every second. Grace enables, supplies, brings forth the gift of righteousness; it restores. This pure grace of God points to Jesus and everything that He is and has done for us. You may be broken, lack confidence, and disappointed about your life. But get ready to shift. You're about to have a head-on collision with the grace of God.

People who lack confidence often feel condemned and put down. But God does not want to condemn you and make you feel bad. Instead He wants to love and embrace you. God's name is love and His address is grace. There is room for you in His family. He is the best at giving confidence. Confidence is so important that you must be willing to fight for it. It is the reverse key to the posture of a victim.

Even though holding on to confidence can at times be a fight, I believe it is one worth fighting. This is not easy because we are in warfare. It is a warfare that breaks forth because of the shift that's taking place in your life. You've rejected darkness and suffering, yet Satan will fight to get you back into a state of bondage or mindset. The enemy fights us in our mind and uses our past and voices of others to shatter our confidence. Oh but for grace. You must understand that you can't defeat an enemy you don't know. We know the enemy hates Grace because it is our strength, present help and supplier.

The enemy of the soul wants to shatter our confidence. He fights against our soul, thoughts, memories, will and emotions, inadequacies, past, present, and future.

The enemy wants us to be distracted away from true confidence. As you know, he is defeated in your life because the Greater One lives in you. Grace drives the devil and his kingdom crazy. Everyday be thankful that we have God's anointing working in our lives to teach us and give to us power over such schemes designed to pull us down into a dark valley.

You are born of God. This means that He has created you to be one of His children. That should give you pure confidence. Through life's development and maturity, God will bring you into increasing confidence where you will experience the fullness of His joy, peace, and holiness to the fullest.

He is abiding within you, living in you, and loving through you so that you are empowered to be His witness. Ephesians states that you should not let darkness return, but instead stay in the light that is shining brightly within you, so walk as children of the light (Eph. 5:8-10).

Of all we can say, the most important is that our confidence must be in the work of cross, the empty tomb and the filling of the Holy Spirit. It may appear a little old school, but, "Thank God for Jesus." It's amazing how things come full circle in life, but as a believer everything starts and ends with Jesus. Everything that we are is through Christ Jesus. The Father loved us so much that He sent His son to save us. So to remain confident, we must hide our lives in Him and abide in Him. Our confidence cannot be in man, money, family, knowledge or anything else.

## From Victim To VICTOR CONFESSION

Today, I decree and declare that I am no longer a victim. I acknowledge that I've been hurt, but today I receive the "Grace of God" for all of my pain. God's grace is my strength that's made perfect in my weakness and for me He is strength like no other (2 Cor. 12:9). Today, I decree and declare that I will not allow the feelings and emotions of the past rob me of my grace future in Christ Jesus. In Christ Jesus I am victorious. I decree and declare that I will not be moved by overwhelming feelings or past failures. God is bigger and more powerful than anything and everything I've ever been through. I walk in the promises God has for me and His Word transforms my mind.

No matter what my situation looks like, I choose to believe God's truth and tear down the devil's lies. I am not defeated. I have set my hope in Jesus, who causes me—we, us—to triumph, (2 Cor. 2:14) and by faith I walk in power and victory as I decree and declare the word of God over my life.

# Conclusion

Welcome to your final stop in this book. I like to call it the dressing room of Grace. I'm sure you've been shopping before, and at some point you've needed to try something on in the dressing room. I've discovered that it does not matter how good an outfit may look, the true test is when you try it on. It is there in the dressing room as you try on the new outfit that you finally get to see how it looks on you. You now have permission to try on "Joy" and see how it looks on you. If you like the way it looks, keep wearing it right out of the dressing room. In fact, carry it with you for the rest of your life and look in the mirror as often as you would like and need. Step-by-step see yourself putting on, Salvation, Peace, Joy, Righteousness, Honor, Love, Wholeness, Strength, Prosperity, Glory, Power, Confidence and Grace. And now you are ready to live.

When this dressing room experience came upon me, I was ready to live. Everywhere I went, I saw freedom. During a recent trip to New Orleans, I noticed that everywhere I looked, the people of New Orleans, were expressing their freedom. Now I believe that true freedom only comes through Jesus Christ; but as I looked around in New Orleans, everyone had a unique expression. Some painted their faces; some wore funny clothes; while others made music on the bottom of buckets. The revelation I received from all of this is that regardless of what happens to you, keep living and smile. Not just waking up and breathing but truly living. I wondered as I observe people, how can people who are in darkness and not know Christ yet be so jubilant?

The better question I asked myself was, "How can people who know Christ be so sad?"

Something is wrong with this picture. I quickly realized that vision, hope, revelation, and joy must be restored among the children of God. We must discover a reason to be joyous and hopeful about our tomorrows, and we can only do it as we grow in a thriving relationship with "Abba Father." Abba Father is just another way of saying, Daddy. It brings us to a new sense of the true joy of a personal relationship with Christ. You were created for the fruit of the spirit to reside in you and that fruit is Love, Joy, Peace, Longsuffering, Gentleness, Goodness, Faith, Meekness and Temperance (Gal. 5:22).

Today, I call you a winner and give you permission to say it out loud, "I am no longer a victim."

# Author's Contact Page

## Charles P. Roberson Sr.

Kingdom Connection Ministries
Kingdom Life Christian Fellowship
Savannah , GA 31406
(912) 921-5346, Office Number
(912) 921-5347, Fax Number

Email
Pastorroberson@gmail.com

Twitter
http://twitter.com/#!/PastorRoberson

Linkedin
http://www.linkedin.com/pub/charles-roberson/12/612/b51